Quantum Computer Vs Traditional Computer

Arief Muinnudin

Published by Arief Muinnudin, 2024.

While every precaution has been taken in the preparation of this book, the publisher assumes no responsibility for errors or omissions, or for damages resulting from the use of the information contained herein.

QUANTUM COMPUTER VS TRADITIONAL COMPUTER

First edition. May 20, 2024.

ISBN: 979-8224017072

Written by Arief Muinnudin.

Table of Contents

Quantum Computer Vs Traditional Computer

Chapter 1: Introduction to Computing

Chapter 2: Foundations of Traditional Computing

Chapter 3: Fundamentals of Quantum Computing

Chapter 4: Computational Models: Classical vs. Quantum

Chapter 5: Processing and Speed: A Comparative Analysis

Chapter 6: Algorithms: Classical and Quantum Perspectives

Chapter 7: Applications of Traditional Computing

Chapter 8: Potential Applications of Quantum Computing

Chapter 9: Hardware and Technical Requirements

Chapter 10: Current State of Technology and Research

Chapter 11: Societal and Ethical Implications

Chapter 12: The Future of Computing: Integration and Evolution

Chapter 13: Preparing for the Quantum Future

Book Summary

Quantum Computer Vs Traditional Computer

Traditional Computers

1. Architecture:

- Traditional computers use bits as the smallest unit of data. A bit can be either 0 or 1.
- They are based on classical binary logic and utilize transistors to perform computations.

2. Processing:

- Perform operations in a sequential manner (though modern CPUs can perform some operations in parallel).
- Use algorithms that follow deterministic paths to solve problems.

3. Speed and Power:

- The speed of traditional computers is limited by the clock speed of the CPU and the efficiency of the algorithms used.
- Can solve many everyday problems efficiently, but struggle with complex problems like large integer factorization or simulations of quantum systems.

4. Applications:

- Used in a wide range of applications including word processing, internet browsing, gaming, data analysis, and more.
- Suitable for tasks requiring precise and repetitive computations.

5. Development and Accessibility:

- Widely developed and accessible to the general public.
- Established technology with extensive software and hardware support.

Quantum Computers

1. Architecture:

- Quantum computers use qubits, which can represent both 0 and 1 simultaneously thanks to the principle of superposition.
- Utilize quantum phenomena such as superposition, entanglement, and quantum tunneling.

2. Processing:

- Perform operations on qubits using quantum gates, which can process many possible states simultaneously.
- Use quantum algorithms that can solve certain problems much faster than classical algorithms (e.g., Shor's algorithm for factoring large numbers, Grover's algorithm for searching unsorted databases).

3. Speed and Power:

- Potentially exponentially faster for specific problems such as cryptography, optimization, and material science simulations.
- Can process complex computations that are infeasible for traditional computers.

4. Applications:

- Currently focused on specialized applications in cryptography, quantum simulations, optimization problems, and drug discovery.

- Not yet suitable for general-purpose computing tasks that traditional computers handle efficiently.

5. Development and Accessibility:

- Still in the experimental and developmental stages with limited availability.
- Requires extremely low temperatures and sophisticated error correction mechanisms.
- Significant ongoing research to improve qubit coherence, error rates, and scalability.

Comparison

Feature	Traditional Computers	Quantum Computers
Basic Unit	Bit (0 or 1)	Qubit (0, 1, or both simultaneously)
Processing	Sequential (parallel in modern CPUs)	Parallel (due to superposition and entanglement)
Speed	Limited by clock speed and classical algorithms	Potentially exponentially faster for specific problems
Applications	General-purpose, everyday tasks	Specialized tasks (cryptography, optimization, etc.)
Development Stage	Mature, widely accessible	Experimental, limited accessibility
Physical Requirements	Room temperature, conventional cooling	Extremely low temperatures, advanced cooling systems

Quantum computers hold the promise of revolutionizing certain fields by solving problems that are currently intractable for traditional computers. However, they are not yet a replacement for classical computers in everyday applications and are primarily a tool for specialized tasks requiring immense computational power.

Chapter 1: Introduction to Computing

1.1 Overview of Traditional Computing

Traditional computing, also known as classical computing, is the backbone of modern technology. It has evolved over decades, transforming from simple mechanical calculators to the sophisticated digital devices that pervade every aspect of our lives today. Understanding the foundations of traditional computing provides a crucial context for exploring the revolutionary potential of quantum computing.

Historical Development

The history of traditional computing can be traced back to ancient times when humans first used tools to aid in calculations. The abacus, one of the earliest known computing devices, was used by various civilizations for arithmetic operations. The development of mechanical calculators in the 17th century by inventors like Blaise Pascal and Gottfried Wilhelm Leibniz marked significant milestones in computing history.

The 19th century saw the advent of more advanced mechanical devices, such as Charles Babbage's Analytical Engine, which laid the groundwork for modern computers. However, it wasn't until the mid-20th century that electronic digital computers began to emerge. The development of the Electronic Numerical Integrator and Computer (ENIAC) during World War II marked the beginning of the electronic computing era.

The subsequent decades witnessed rapid advancements in computing technology. The invention of the transistor in 1947 and the integrated circuit in 1958 revolutionized computer design, leading to smaller, faster, and more reliable machines. The 1970s and 1980s saw the rise of personal computers, with companies like Apple and IBM playing pivotal roles in bringing computing power to the masses.

Basic Principles and Architecture

At the core of traditional computing lies the von Neumann architecture, named after mathematician John von Neumann. This architecture consists of a central processing unit (CPU), memory, and input/output (I/O) devices. The CPU, often referred to as the brain of the computer, executes instructions stored in memory. Memory is used to store data and program instructions temporarily or permanently, while I/O devices facilitate communication between the computer and the external world.

Traditional computers operate on binary logic, where data is represented using bits—binary digits that can be either 0 or 1. This binary system is the foundation of all classical computing operations. Boolean logic, named after mathematician George Boole, is used to perform logical operations on binary data, enabling the execution of complex computations.

Key Components: CPU, Memory, Storage, and I/O Devices

- **CPU (Central Processing Unit)**: The CPU is responsible for executing instructions and performing calculations. It consists of an arithmetic logic unit (ALU) for mathematical operations, a control unit (CU) for instruction decoding, and registers for temporary data storage.
- **Memory**: Memory can be classified into volatile memory (e.g., RAM) and non-volatile memory (e.g., ROM, hard drives, SSDs). RAM (Random Access Memory) provides temporary storage for data and instructions that the CPU needs to access quickly. Non-volatile memory retains data even when the computer is powered off.
- **Storage**: Long-term storage devices, such as hard drives and solid-state drives (SSDs), store data permanently. These devices offer large storage capacities and are essential for maintaining

operating systems, applications, and user data.

- **I/O Devices**: Input devices, such as keyboards and mice, allow users to interact with the computer. Output devices, such as monitors and printers, enable the computer to communicate results to the user. Peripheral devices, like USB drives and external hard drives, expand the computer's functionality.

1.2 Introduction to Quantum Computing

Quantum computing represents a paradigm shift in the field of computation, harnessing the principles of quantum mechanics to process information in fundamentally new ways. While traditional computers rely on bits, quantum computers use qubits, which can exist in multiple states simultaneously, offering the potential for unprecedented computational power.

Definition and Scope of Quantum Computing

Quantum computing leverages the unique properties of quantum mechanics, such as superposition and entanglement, to perform calculations that are infeasible for classical computers. Unlike classical bits, which are either 0 or 1, qubits can exist in a superposition of both states, enabling parallelism at a scale unimaginable in traditional computing.

The scope of quantum computing extends far beyond mere speed improvements. It promises to revolutionize fields such as cryptography, optimization, material science, and drug discovery by solving complex problems more efficiently than classical computers. Quantum computers could potentially crack current encryption schemes, optimize large-scale systems, simulate quantum phenomena, and accelerate scientific discoveries.

Early Theoretical Foundations and Pioneers in the Field

The theoretical foundations of quantum computing were laid in the early 20th century with the development of quantum mechanics. Key figures such as Max Planck, Albert Einstein, Niels Bohr, and Erwin Schrödinger made significant contributions to the understanding of quantum phenomena.

The concept of quantum computing was first proposed by physicist Richard Feynman in 1982. Feynman suggested that simulating quantum systems on classical computers was inefficient and proposed the idea of using quantum systems themselves for computation. David Deutsch further developed this idea in 1985 by introducing the concept of a universal quantum computer, capable of performing any computation that a classical computer can, but potentially much faster.

The Journey from Theoretical Physics to Practical Quantum Computers

The journey from theoretical physics to practical quantum computers has been marked by numerous milestones. In the 1990s, Peter Shor developed a quantum algorithm for factoring large numbers exponentially faster than the best-known classical algorithms, highlighting the potential of quantum computing for cryptography. Lov Grover introduced a quantum search algorithm that could search unsorted databases more efficiently than classical algorithms.

Experimental efforts to build quantum computers began to gain momentum in the late 20th and early 21st centuries. Researchers developed various qubit technologies, including superconducting qubits, trapped ions, and photonic qubits. Companies like IBM, Google, and Microsoft, as well as numerous academic institutions, have made significant strides in building and scaling quantum processors.

Despite the progress, quantum computing is still in its early stages, with many technical challenges remaining. Researchers continue to work on improving qubit coherence, error correction, and scalability to realize the full potential of quantum computing.

1.3 Importance of Comparing the Two Paradigms

Understanding both traditional and quantum computing paradigms is crucial for several reasons. As quantum computing continues to advance, it is essential to appreciate its potential impact on various industries, the broader implications for science and technology, and the ethical considerations that arise from its development and deployment.

Why Understanding Both Paradigms is Crucial for Future Technological Advancements

Traditional computing has been the cornerstone of technological advancements for decades, driving innovation in fields such as artificial intelligence, data science, and cloud computing. However, as we approach the physical limits of classical computing, quantum computing offers a new frontier for breakthroughs in computational power and efficiency.

By comparing traditional and quantum computing, we can better understand the unique strengths and limitations of each paradigm. This knowledge is essential for developing hybrid systems that leverage the best of both worlds, enabling new applications and solving problems that are currently intractable.

The Potential Implications for Various Industries

The impact of quantum computing extends across multiple industries. In finance, quantum algorithms could optimize portfolios, detect fraud, and perform complex risk assessments. In logistics, quantum computing could enhance supply chain management and route optimization. In healthcare, it could accelerate drug discovery and improve personalized medicine.

The potential implications for cybersecurity are particularly significant. Quantum computers could break existing encryption schemes, necessitating the development of quantum-resistant cryptographic methods. At the same time, quantum cryptography offers new ways to secure communications, ensuring data privacy and integrity.

The Broader Impact on Science, Technology, and Society

The broader impact of quantum computing on science and technology cannot be overstated. Quantum simulations could provide deeper insights into fundamental physical processes, leading to advancements in material science, chemistry, and physics. These insights could, in turn, drive technological innovations in areas such as energy, manufacturing, and environmental sustainability.

From a societal perspective, the advent of quantum computing raises important ethical considerations. Ensuring equitable access to quantum technology, addressing potential job displacement, and navigating the balance between security and privacy are critical issues that must be addressed. By understanding the differences and potential synergies between traditional and quantum computing, we can better prepare for the transformative changes that lie ahead.

Chapter 2: Foundations of Traditional Computing

2.1 Historical Development

The development of traditional computing spans centuries, marked by incremental advancements and revolutionary breakthroughs. Understanding this historical context provides a foundation for appreciating the capabilities and limitations of classical computers.

The Origins of Computing: From Abacuses to Early Mechanical Calculators

The history of computing can be traced back to ancient civilizations that used tools like the abacus for arithmetic operations. The abacus, used by cultures such as the Babylonians, Chinese, and Greeks, is one of the earliest known computing devices, enabling users to perform basic calculations efficiently.

In the 17th century, mechanical calculators began to emerge. Blaise Pascal invented the Pascaline, a mechanical calculator capable of performing addition and subtraction. Gottfried Wilhelm Leibniz improved upon Pascal's design with the Leibniz Wheel, which could perform multiplication and division. These early devices laid the groundwork for future developments in computing technology.

The Advent of Electronic Computing: ENIAC and Beyond

The 20th century saw the advent of electronic computing, revolutionizing the field with machines capable of performing complex calculations at unprecedented speeds. During World War II, the development of the Electronic Numerical Integrator and Computer (ENIAC) marked a significant milestone. ENIAC, built by John Presper

Eckert and John Mauchly, was the first general-purpose electronic digital computer, capable of solving a wide range of computational problems.

The development of the transistor in 1947 by John Bardeen, Walter Brattain, and William Shockley at Bell Labs was another pivotal moment. Transistors replaced vacuum tubes, making computers smaller, faster, and more reliable. The invention of the integrated circuit in 1958 by Jack Kilby and Robert Noyce further miniaturized electronic components, leading to the development of microprocessors.

The Rise of Personal Computers and the Internet Revolution

The 1970s and 1980s saw the rise of personal computers, bringing computing power to individuals and small businesses. The introduction of the Altair 8800 in 1975, followed by the Apple II in 1977 and the IBM PC in 1981, democratized access to computing technology. These developments were accompanied by the creation of user-friendly operating systems and software applications, making computers more accessible to the general public.

The internet revolution in the 1990s transformed traditional computing by connecting computers worldwide, enabling the exchange of information and the development of new services and applications. The World Wide Web, invented by Tim Berners-Lee in 1989, became a catalyst for the digital age, driving innovation in communication, commerce, and entertainment.

2.2 Basic Principles and Architecture

The basic principles and architecture of traditional computing are rooted in the von Neumann architecture, which defines the structure and operation of classical computers. This architecture consists of a central processing unit (CPU), memory, and input/output (I/O) devices, all interconnected by a system bus.

The Binary System and Boolean Logic

Traditional computers operate on the binary system, where data is represented using bits—binary digits that can be either 0 or 1. This binary system forms the basis of all classical computing operations. Boolean logic, named after mathematician George Boole, is used to perform logical operations on binary data. Boolean operations, such as AND, OR, and NOT, are fundamental to the functioning of digital circuits and processors.

The von Neumann Architecture: CPU, Memory, and Storage

The von Neumann architecture, proposed by John von Neumann in the 1940s, defines the basic structure of a classical computer. This architecture includes:

- **CPU (Central Processing Unit)**: The CPU is the brain of the computer, responsible for executing instructions and performing calculations. It consists of an arithmetic logic unit (ALU) for mathematical operations, a control unit (CU) for instruction decoding, and registers for temporary data storage.
- **Memory**: Memory is used to store data and program instructions. It can be classified into volatile memory (e.g., RAM) and non-volatile memory (e.g., ROM, hard drives, SSDs). RAM (Random Access Memory) provides temporary storage for data and instructions that the CPU needs to access quickly. Non-volatile memory retains data even when the computer is powered off.
- **Storage**: Long-term storage devices, such as hard drives and solid-state drives (SSDs), store data permanently. These devices offer large storage capacities and are essential for maintaining operating systems, applications, and user data.
- **I/O Devices**: Input devices, such as keyboards and mice, allow

users to interact with the computer. Output devices, such as monitors and printers, enable the computer to communicate results to the user. Peripheral devices, like USB drives and external hard drives, expand the computer's functionality.

The Role of Operating Systems and Software in Classical Computing

Operating systems (OS) play a crucial role in managing computer hardware and software resources. The OS provides an interface between the user and the hardware, enabling efficient execution of programs and management of system resources. Popular operating systems, such as Windows, macOS, and Linux, offer a wide range of functionalities, including multitasking, file management, and security features.

Software applications, ranging from word processors to complex databases, run on top of the operating system, enabling users to perform specific tasks. The development of software programming languages, such as C, Java, and Python, has facilitated the creation of diverse and powerful applications, driving innovation in various fields.

2.3 Key Components: CPU, Memory, Storage, and I/O Devices

CPU (Central Processing Unit)

The CPU is the core component of a traditional computer, responsible for executing instructions and performing calculations. It consists of several key elements:

- **Arithmetic Logic Unit (ALU):** The ALU performs arithmetic operations (addition, subtraction, multiplication, division) and logical operations (AND, OR, NOT, XOR) on binary data.
- **Control Unit (CU):** The CU decodes program instructions and controls the execution of operations within the CPU. It manages the flow of data between the CPU, memory, and I/O

devices.

- **Registers**: Registers are small, fast storage locations within the CPU that hold data temporarily during processing. They are used to store intermediate results, addresses, and instructions.

Memory

Memory in traditional computers is categorized into two main types: volatile and non-volatile memory.

- **Volatile Memory**: RAM (Random Access Memory) is a type of volatile memory that provides temporary storage for data and instructions that the CPU needs to access quickly. RAM is essential for running applications and performing tasks efficiently.
- **Non-Volatile Memory**: Non-volatile memory, such as ROM (Read-Only Memory), hard drives, and solid-state drives (SSDs), retains data even when the computer is powered off. ROM stores firmware and system-level instructions, while hard drives and SSDs provide long-term storage for operating systems, applications, and user data.

Storage

Storage devices in traditional computers provide long-term data storage and retrieval. The two main types of storage devices are:

- **Hard Drives**: Hard disk drives (HDDs) use spinning magnetic disks to store data. They offer large storage capacities at relatively low costs but are slower and more prone to mechanical failures compared to SSDs.
- **Solid-State Drives (SSDs)**: SSDs use flash memory to store data, offering faster read/write speeds and greater reliability

than HDDs. They are more expensive per gigabyte but provide significant performance improvements.

I/O Devices

Input/output (I/O) devices enable users to interact with the computer and facilitate communication between the computer and external systems.

- **Input Devices**: Keyboards, mice, and touchscreens allow users to input data and commands into the computer. Scanners and cameras capture images and documents for processing.
- **Output Devices**: Monitors, printers, and speakers output data and results from the computer to the user. Displays provide visual feedback, while printers produce physical copies of documents.
- **Peripheral Devices**: External storage devices, such as USB drives and external hard drives, expand the computer's storage capacity. Networking devices, such as modems and routers, enable internet connectivity and data transfer between computers.

By understanding the key components and architecture of traditional computing, we gain a comprehensive foundation for exploring the revolutionary potential of quantum computing. In the following chapters, we will delve into the principles of quantum computing, comparing and contrasting it with classical computing to highlight the unique advantages and challenges of each paradigm.

Chapter 3: Fundamentals of Quantum Computing

3.1 Historical Context and Key Milestones

Quantum computing, rooted in the principles of quantum mechanics, represents a groundbreaking shift from classical computing. Its development has been driven by both theoretical advancements and experimental achievements.

Early Theoretical Foundations

The early 20th century saw the birth of quantum mechanics, with pioneering work by physicists such as Max Planck, Albert Einstein, Niels Bohr, and Erwin Schrödinger. Their discoveries revealed the peculiar and counterintuitive nature of subatomic particles, laying the groundwork for quantum computing.

The Concept of Quantum Computing

In 1982, Richard Feynman proposed the idea of a quantum computer, capable of simulating quantum systems more efficiently than classical computers. This marked the inception of quantum computing as a theoretical concept. David Deutsch further developed this idea in 1985, introducing the notion of a universal quantum computer.

Key Milestones in Quantum Computing

- **1994**: Peter Shor developed Shor's algorithm, demonstrating that a quantum computer could factor large numbers exponentially faster than the best-known classical algorithms. This breakthrough highlighted the potential of quantum computing for cryptography.
- **1996**: Lov Grover introduced Grover's algorithm, which could

search unsorted databases quadratically faster than classical algorithms, showcasing another significant advantage of quantum computing.

- **2019**: Google claimed quantum supremacy with its quantum processor, Sycamore, by performing a specific calculation faster than the most powerful classical supercomputer at the time. This milestone underscored the practical potential of quantum computing.

3.2 Quantum Mechanics Principles: Superposition, Entanglement, and Quantum Tunneling

Quantum computing harnesses the unique properties of quantum mechanics to perform computations. Understanding these principles is crucial to grasp how quantum computers operate.

Superposition

Superposition is the ability of a quantum system to exist in multiple states simultaneously. Unlike classical bits, which are either 0 or 1, qubits can be in a superposition of both states. This property allows quantum computers to process a vast amount of information in parallel, significantly enhancing computational power.

Entanglement

Entanglement is a phenomenon where quantum particles become interconnected, such that the state of one particle instantly influences the state of another, regardless of the distance between them. This interconnectedness enables qubits to work together in ways that classical bits cannot, allowing for more complex and efficient computations.

Quantum Tunneling

Quantum tunneling is the ability of a particle to pass through a potential barrier that it classically should not be able to cross. This phenomenon can be exploited in quantum computing to solve problems more efficiently, as it allows quantum particles to explore multiple pathways simultaneously.

3.3 Basic Components: Qubits, Quantum Gates, and Quantum Circuits

Quantum computers are built on a foundation of unique components that differ significantly from those in classical computers.

Qubits

Qubits are the fundamental units of quantum information. They can exist in a superposition of states, enabling parallel processing. Various physical systems can be used to create qubits, including:

- **Superconducting Qubits**: These use superconducting circuits cooled to near absolute zero to create and manipulate qubits.
- **Trapped Ions**: Ions are trapped and manipulated using electromagnetic fields, allowing for precise control of qubit states.
- **Photonic Qubits**: Photons are used to represent qubits, with quantum states encoded in their polarization or phase.

Quantum Gates

Quantum gates manipulate the states of qubits, analogous to classical logic gates. However, quantum gates operate on the principles of quantum mechanics, allowing for operations like superposition and entanglement. Common quantum gates include:

- **Hadamard Gate (H)**: Creates a superposition state from a classical state.

- **Pauli-X Gate**: Flips the state of a qubit, similar to a classical NOT gate.
- **CNOT Gate**: Entangles two qubits, flipping the state of the second qubit if the first qubit is in the state $|1\rangle$.

Quantum Circuits

Quantum circuits consist of qubits and quantum gates arranged to perform specific computations. Quantum algorithms are implemented using these circuits, with qubits passing through a series of gates to achieve the desired outcome.

3.4 Bit vs. Qubit: The Core Difference

The fundamental difference between classical bits and qubits lies in their representation and capabilities.

Understanding Classical Bits

Classical bits are binary units of information that can be either 0 or 1. Classical computers perform computations by manipulating these bits using logical operations. Each bit can only represent one state at a time, limiting the parallelism in classical computations.

Exploring Qubits and Their Unique Properties

Qubits, on the other hand, can exist in a superposition of states, allowing them to represent both 0 and 1 simultaneously. This property enables quantum computers to perform many calculations at once, exponentially increasing their computational power for certain tasks.

The Impact of Superposition and Entanglement on Computation

Superposition allows quantum computers to process multiple possibilities simultaneously, while entanglement enables qubits to work together in ways that classical bits cannot. These properties allow quantum algorithms to solve problems more efficiently than classical algorithms, particularly for tasks involving large datasets and complex computations.

Chapter 4: Computational Models: Classical vs. Quantum

4.1 Turing Machines and Classical Algorithms

The classical computational model is based on Turing machines and well-established algorithms.

Turing Machines

A Turing machine, conceptualized by Alan Turing in 1936, is an abstract computational model that defines a machine capable of performing any computation through a sequence of operations on an infinite tape. This model forms the theoretical foundation of classical computing, demonstrating the limits of what can be computed.

Classical Algorithms

Classical algorithms are step-by-step procedures for solving computational problems. They are executed sequentially on classical computers, with each step manipulating binary data. Classical algorithms include sorting, searching, and arithmetic operations, which have been optimized over decades to run efficiently on classical hardware.

4.2 Quantum Turing Machines and Quantum Algorithms

Quantum computing introduces a new computational model based on quantum Turing machines and quantum algorithms.

Quantum Turing Machines

A quantum Turing machine extends the classical Turing machine model to incorporate the principles of quantum mechanics. It operates on qubits and uses quantum gates to perform computations. This model demonstrates the theoretical capabilities of quantum computers, including their ability to solve certain problems more efficiently than classical computers.

Quantum Algorithms

Quantum algorithms leverage the properties of quantum mechanics to achieve computational speedups. Notable quantum algorithms include:

- **Shor's Algorithm**: Efficiently factors large numbers, posing a threat to classical cryptographic schemes.
- **Grover's Algorithm**: Performs database searches quadratically faster than classical algorithms.
- **Quantum Fourier Transform (QFT)**: Underlies many quantum algorithms, enabling efficient solutions to problems in signal processing and cryptography.

4.3 Key Differences in Problem-Solving Approaches

The differences in computational models lead to distinct approaches to problem-solving in classical and quantum computing.

Classical Problem-Solving

Classical algorithms solve problems through sequential and parallel processing, leveraging optimized techniques for specific tasks. These algorithms have been refined over time to handle a wide range of applications efficiently.

Quantum Problem-Solving

Quantum algorithms exploit superposition and entanglement to explore multiple solutions simultaneously. This parallelism allows quantum computers to solve certain problems more efficiently than classical computers, particularly those involving large search spaces or complex mathematical structures.

Comparative Analysis

While classical computers excel at tasks involving well-defined, sequential computations, quantum computers offer significant advantages for problems requiring extensive parallel processing and complex mathematical operations. Understanding the strengths and limitations of each approach is crucial for developing hybrid systems that combine the best of both worlds.

Chapter 5: Processing and Speed: A Comparative Analysis

5.1 Classical Processing: Sequential and Parallel Computing

Classical computing relies on both sequential and parallel processing techniques to execute tasks efficiently.

Sequential Processing

In sequential processing, tasks are executed one after another in a linear fashion. This approach is straightforward and effective for many applications, but it can be slow for complex computations that require significant processing power.

Parallel Computing

Parallel computing involves dividing tasks into smaller sub-tasks that can be executed simultaneously on multiple processors. This approach enhances computational speed and efficiency, enabling classical computers to handle large-scale problems more effectively. Techniques such as multi-threading and distributed computing are commonly used in parallel processing.

5.2 Quantum Processing: Parallelism Through Superposition

Quantum processing leverages the principles of superposition and entanglement to achieve unparalleled parallelism.

Superposition and Parallelism

Superposition allows qubits to exist in multiple states simultaneously, enabling quantum computers to process a vast number of possibilities in parallel. This inherent parallelism provides a significant speed advantage for certain types of computations, such as searching large datasets or solving complex optimization problems.

Entanglement and Coordination

Entanglement enables qubits to work together in ways that classical bits cannot. This coordination allows quantum algorithms to perform complex computations more efficiently, further enhancing the speed and capability of quantum computers.

5.3 Performance Benchmarks and Potential Speed Advantages

The performance of quantum computers can be benchmarked against classical computers to highlight their potential speed advantages.

Classical Performance Benchmarks

Classical computers are benchmarked using metrics such as clock speed, FLOPS (floating-point operations per second), and latency. These metrics provide a measure of the computational power and efficiency of classical systems.

Quantum Performance Benchmarks

Quantum computers are benchmarked using metrics such as qubit count, coherence time, and quantum volume. Quantum volume, in particular, measures the overall performance of a quantum computer, taking into account the number of qubits, error rates, and gate fidelity.

Comparative Analysis

Quantum computers have demonstrated significant speed advantages for specific tasks, such as factoring large numbers (Shor's algorithm) and searching unsorted databases (Grover's algorithm). However, classical computers still outperform quantum computers in many everyday applications. The ongoing development of quantum hardware and algorithms aims to expand the range of problems where quantum computers can achieve a clear advantage.

Chapter 6: Algorithms: Classical and Quantum Perspectives

6.1 Overview of Classical Algorithms

Classical algorithms form the backbone of traditional computing, solving a wide range of problems efficiently.

Sorting Algorithms

Sorting algorithms, such as quicksort, mergesort, and heapsort, arrange data in a specific order, enabling efficient data retrieval and manipulation.

Searching Algorithms

Searching algorithms, including binary search and linear search, locate specific elements within datasets. These algorithms are optimized for speed and accuracy.

Optimization Algorithms

Optimization algorithms, such as dynamic programming and greedy algorithms, solve complex problems by finding the best solution among many possible options. Applications include resource allocation, scheduling, and route planning.

6.2 Introduction to Quantum Algorithms

Quantum algorithms leverage the principles of quantum mechanics to achieve computational speedups.

Shor's Algorithm

Shor's algorithm efficiently factors large numbers, providing an exponential speedup over classical algorithms. This breakthrough has significant implications for cryptography, as many encryption schemes rely on the difficulty of factoring large numbers.

Grover's Algorithm

Grover's algorithm searches unsorted databases quadratically faster than classical algorithms. This speedup is valuable for a wide range of applications, from database searches to cryptographic analysis.

Quantum Fourier Transform (QFT)

The Quantum Fourier Transform (QFT) is a key component of many quantum algorithms, enabling efficient solutions to problems in signal processing, cryptography, and more. QFT provides an exponential speedup over classical Fourier transforms for specific tasks.

6.3 Comparative Efficiency and Real-World Implications

The efficiency of quantum algorithms compared to classical algorithms has significant real-world implications.

Efficiency Analysis

Quantum algorithms offer exponential or quadratic speedups for specific problems, providing a clear advantage over classical algorithms. These speedups can revolutionize fields such as cryptography, optimization, and scientific research.

Real-World Applications

The real-world implications of quantum algorithms are vast. In cryptography, quantum algorithms threaten the security of classical encryption schemes, necessitating the development of quantum-resistant algorithms. In optimization, quantum algorithms can solve complex logistical problems more efficiently, impacting industries such as finance, transportation, and manufacturing. Scientific research can benefit from quantum simulations, enabling breakthroughs in material science, drug discovery, and fundamental physics.

Chapter 7: Applications of Traditional Computing

7.1 Everyday Applications: Personal Computing, Business, Entertainment

Traditional computing has become integral to everyday life, with applications spanning personal computing, business, and entertainment.

Personal Computing

Personal computers (PCs) are ubiquitous, used for tasks such as web browsing, word processing, and gaming. Operating systems like Windows, macOS, and Linux provide user-friendly interfaces and a wide range of functionalities.

Business Applications

Businesses rely on traditional computing for a variety of tasks, including data management, communication, and financial transactions. Enterprise software, such as customer relationship management (CRM) systems and enterprise resource planning (ERP) systems, streamline business operations and improve efficiency.

Entertainment

The entertainment industry has been transformed by traditional computing, with applications in digital media, video games, and streaming services. High-performance computers enable the creation and delivery of rich, interactive content, enhancing user experiences.

7.2 High-Performance Computing: Scientific Simulations, Data Analysis

High-performance computing (HPC) extends the capabilities of traditional computing to solve complex problems in scientific research and data analysis.

Scientific Simulations

HPC systems perform simulations of physical, chemical, and biological processes, enabling researchers to study phenomena that are difficult or impossible to observe directly. Applications include climate modeling, astrophysics, and molecular dynamics.

Data Analysis

HPC systems analyze vast datasets, uncovering patterns and insights that drive innovation in fields such as genomics, finance, and artificial intelligence. Techniques such as machine learning and data mining are employed to extract valuable information from large-scale data.

7.3 Limitations and Challenges Faced by Traditional Computers

Despite their widespread use, traditional computers face limitations and challenges.

Scalability Issues

As data volumes grow, traditional computers struggle to scale efficiently. Processing large datasets and performing complex computations require significant resources, leading to bottlenecks and performance constraints.

Energy Consumption

High-performance computing systems consume substantial amounts of energy, raising concerns about sustainability and operational costs. Improving energy efficiency is a key challenge for the future of traditional computing.

Security Vulnerabilities

Traditional computers are vulnerable to security threats, including malware, hacking, and data breaches. Ensuring data security and protecting sensitive information remain critical concerns.

By understanding the strengths, applications, and limitations of traditional computing, we can better appreciate the potential of quantum computing to address these challenges and revolutionize the field of computing. In the following chapters, we will explore the potential applications and implications of quantum computing, providing a comprehensive comparison with traditional computing.

Chapter 8: Potential Applications of Quantum Computing

8.1 Cryptography and Security: Breaking Classical Encryption, Quantum Encryption

Quantum computing has significant implications for cryptography and security, potentially transforming how we protect data and communications.

Breaking Classical Encryption

Quantum computers pose a threat to classical encryption methods, particularly those based on the difficulty of factoring large numbers or solving discrete logarithm problems. Shor's algorithm, for example, can factor large integers exponentially faster than the best classical algorithms, compromising widely-used encryption schemes such as RSA and ECC (Elliptic Curve Cryptography). This potential capability necessitates the development of new cryptographic techniques that can withstand quantum attacks.

Quantum Encryption

Quantum computing also offers new methods for securing data through quantum encryption. Quantum key distribution (QKD) leverages the principles of quantum mechanics, such as superposition and entanglement, to create encryption keys that are theoretically secure against any computational attack. QKD enables the exchange of encryption keys in a manner that guarantees the detection of any eavesdropping, providing an unprecedented level of security for sensitive communications.

8.2 Optimization Problems: Logistics, Finance, Machine Learning

Quantum computing has the potential to revolutionize the way we solve complex optimization problems across various industries.

Logistics

In logistics, optimizing routes, schedules, and resource allocation are crucial for efficiency and cost reduction. Quantum algorithms can solve these optimization problems more effectively than classical algorithms, finding the best solutions in significantly less time. This capability can lead to more efficient transportation networks, supply chain management, and delivery systems.

Finance

The financial industry can benefit from quantum computing in portfolio optimization, risk assessment, and fraud detection. Quantum algorithms can analyze vast amounts of data and identify optimal investment strategies more quickly and accurately than classical methods. Additionally, quantum computing can enhance the modeling of complex financial systems, leading to better decision-making and risk management.

Machine Learning

Machine learning algorithms, particularly those used in deep learning and neural networks, require substantial computational resources. Quantum computing can accelerate these algorithms by providing faster solutions to optimization problems inherent in training models. This capability can improve the performance and efficiency of machine learning applications, enabling advancements in areas such as image recognition, natural language processing, and predictive analytics.

8.3 Scientific Research: Quantum Simulations, Drug Discovery, Material Science

Quantum computing holds promise for advancing scientific research by enabling simulations and discoveries that are beyond the reach of classical computers.

Quantum Simulations

Quantum simulations allow researchers to model complex quantum systems accurately. This capability is particularly valuable in fields such as quantum chemistry and condensed matter physics, where understanding the behavior of molecules and materials at the quantum level is essential. Quantum simulations can lead to new insights into chemical reactions, phase transitions, and other fundamental processes.

Drug Discovery

In drug discovery, quantum computing can accelerate the identification of potential drug candidates by simulating molecular interactions more accurately than classical methods. This capability can reduce the time and cost associated with drug development, leading to more effective treatments for diseases. Quantum algorithms can also optimize the design of new drugs, improving their efficacy and safety.

Material Science

Quantum computing can revolutionize material science by enabling the discovery of new materials with unique properties. By simulating the behavior of atoms and electrons in different configurations, researchers can identify materials with desirable characteristics, such as high conductivity, strength, or light absorption. These discoveries can lead to advancements in technology, energy storage, and manufacturing.

Chapter 9: Hardware and Technical Requirements

9.1 Traditional Computer Hardware: Transistors, Integrated Circuits, Moore's Law

Traditional computer hardware has evolved significantly, driven by advances in semiconductor technology and the principles of Moore's Law.

Transistors and Integrated Circuits

Transistors are the fundamental building blocks of traditional computer hardware. These semiconductor devices control the flow of electrical current, enabling the execution of binary operations. Integrated circuits (ICs), which contain millions of transistors on a single chip, have allowed for the miniaturization and increased performance of computer systems.

Moore's Law

Moore's Law, articulated by Gordon Moore in 1965, states that the number of transistors on a microchip doubles approximately every two years, leading to exponential increases in computing power. While this trend has driven the rapid advancement of traditional computing technology, it faces physical and economic limits as transistors approach the size of atoms.

9.2 Quantum Hardware: Qubits, Quantum Processors, Error Correction

Quantum computing hardware is fundamentally different from traditional hardware, relying on qubits and specialized quantum processors.

Qubits

Qubits are the basic units of quantum information, capable of representing both 0 and 1 simultaneously due to superposition. Various physical systems, such as superconducting circuits, trapped ions, and photons, can be used to create and manipulate qubits. Each type of qubit has its advantages and challenges in terms of coherence time, scalability, and error rates.

Quantum Processors

Quantum processors, or quantum processing units (QPUs), perform computations by applying quantum gates to qubits. These processors are designed to execute quantum algorithms and require highly controlled environments to maintain qubit coherence and minimize errors. Leading companies, such as IBM, Google, and Intel, are developing quantum processors with increasing numbers of qubits and improved performance.

Error Correction

Quantum error correction is essential for reliable quantum computing, as qubits are highly susceptible to errors from decoherence and quantum noise. Quantum error correction codes, such as the surface code, enable the detection and correction of errors in qubit states. Implementing effective error correction requires additional qubits and sophisticated algorithms, posing a significant challenge for scaling up quantum computers.

9.3 Challenges in Developing and Maintaining Quantum Computers

The development and maintenance of quantum computers involve numerous technical and practical challenges.

Scalability

Scaling up quantum computers to support a large number of qubits while maintaining low error rates is a significant challenge. Current quantum processors are limited in size and coherence time, requiring advancements in qubit technology and error correction to achieve practical, large-scale quantum computing.

Decoherence and Noise

Qubits are highly sensitive to their environment, with interactions causing decoherence and introducing noise. Maintaining qubit coherence and minimizing noise are critical for accurate quantum computations. This requires sophisticated isolation techniques, cryogenic cooling, and error correction methods.

Cost and Infrastructure

Building and maintaining quantum computers is expensive, requiring specialized equipment, materials, and facilities. The need for cryogenic temperatures, vacuum systems, and high-precision control adds to the complexity and cost. Developing cost-effective and scalable quantum hardware is essential for the widespread adoption of quantum computing.

Chapter 10: Current State of Technology and Research

10.1 Advances in Traditional Computing: AI, Machine Learning, Cloud Computing

Traditional computing continues to advance, driven by innovations in artificial intelligence (AI), machine learning, and cloud computing.

Artificial Intelligence and Machine Learning

AI and machine learning have transformed various industries by enabling systems to learn from data and make intelligent decisions. Advances in algorithms, such as deep learning, have led to breakthroughs in natural language processing, image recognition, and autonomous systems. Traditional computing hardware, including GPUs and TPUs, is optimized for these applications, enhancing their performance and scalability.

Cloud Computing

Cloud computing provides on-demand access to computing resources over the internet, enabling scalable and flexible computing solutions. Cloud platforms, such as Amazon Web Services (AWS), Microsoft Azure, and Google Cloud, offer a wide range of services, including data storage, machine learning, and high-performance computing. The cloud computing paradigm has democratized access to advanced computing capabilities, fostering innovation and collaboration.

10.2 Current State of Quantum Computing: Leading Companies, Experimental Achievements

Quantum computing is an active area of research and development, with significant progress made by leading companies and research institutions.

Leading Companies

Several companies are at the forefront of quantum computing research, including:

- **IBM**: IBM's quantum computing initiative, IBM Q, provides access to quantum processors through the IBM Quantum Experience platform. IBM has made significant advancements in quantum hardware, software, and algorithms.
- **Google**: Google's quantum computing division, Google AI Quantum, achieved a milestone in 2019 by claiming quantum supremacy with its Sycamore processor. Google continues to develop quantum hardware and explore applications of quantum computing.
- **Intel**: Intel is developing quantum processors and exploring new qubit technologies, such as spin qubits and silicon-based qubits. Intel's research focuses on scalability and integration with traditional semiconductor manufacturing processes.
- **Microsoft**: Microsoft's Quantum Development Kit and Azure Quantum platform provide tools and resources for quantum computing research and development. Microsoft is exploring topological qubits as a potential path to scalable quantum computing.

Experimental Achievements

Significant experimental achievements in quantum computing include demonstrations of quantum supremacy, advancements in quantum error correction, and the development of quantum algorithms with practical applications. These achievements highlight the potential of quantum computing and drive ongoing research efforts.

10.3 Major Research Initiatives and Future Prospects

Major research initiatives and collaborative efforts are advancing the field of quantum computing, with promising future prospects.

Research Initiatives

Research initiatives, such as the European Quantum Flagship, the U.S. National Quantum Initiative, and China's Quantum Experiments at Space Scale (QUESS) project, aim to accelerate quantum computing research and development. These initiatives provide funding, resources, and collaboration opportunities for scientists and engineers working on quantum technologies.

Future Prospects

The future of quantum computing holds exciting possibilities, including breakthroughs in cryptography, optimization, and scientific research. As quantum hardware and algorithms continue to improve, the practical applications of quantum computing will expand, potentially revolutionizing various fields and industries.

Chapter 11: Societal and Ethical Implications

11.1 Impact of Traditional Computing on Society: Jobs, Privacy, Digital Divide

Traditional computing has had a profound impact on society, influencing jobs, privacy, and the digital divide.

Jobs

The rise of traditional computing has created new job opportunities in fields such as software development, IT support, data analysis, and cybersecurity. However, it has also led to the automation of many tasks, displacing certain types of jobs and requiring workers to adapt to new skillsets.

Privacy

The widespread use of traditional computing and digital technologies has raised concerns about privacy. The collection and analysis of personal data by companies and governments pose risks to individual privacy and security. Ensuring data protection and implementing robust privacy policies are critical to addressing these concerns.

Digital Divide

The digital divide refers to the gap between individuals and communities with access to modern computing technologies and those without. This divide can exacerbate social and economic inequalities, limiting opportunities for education, employment, and civic participation. Efforts to bridge the digital divide include expanding internet access, providing digital literacy education, and ensuring affordable computing devices.

11.2 Potential Societal Impact of Quantum Computing: Data Security, Economic Shifts

Quantum computing has the potential to bring about significant societal changes, particularly in data security and economic dynamics.

Data Security

Quantum computing's ability to break classical encryption poses a risk to data security, necessitating the development of quantum-resistant cryptographic methods. Conversely, quantum encryption can provide unprecedented levels of security for communications and data, enhancing privacy and protection against cyber threats.

Economic Shifts

Quantum computing can drive economic shifts by enabling new technologies and industries. Sectors such as pharmaceuticals, materials science, and logistics may experience transformative changes, leading to new business models and opportunities. However, these shifts may also disrupt existing industries and job markets, requiring adaptation and workforce retraining.

11.3 Ethical Considerations in the Development and Deployment of Quantum Technology

The development and deployment of quantum technology raise several ethical considerations that must be addressed to ensure responsible innovation.

Equity and Access

Ensuring equitable access to quantum computing resources and benefits is crucial to preventing the exacerbation of existing inequalities. Policies and initiatives should promote inclusivity and address the needs of underrepresented communities in the quantum computing ecosystem.

Security and Privacy

The potential for quantum computing to break classical encryption necessitates a careful consideration of security and privacy implications. Researchers and policymakers must collaborate to develop quantum-resistant cryptographic methods and frameworks to protect sensitive information.

Ethical Use of Quantum Technology

The ethical use of quantum technology involves considering its potential impacts on society, the environment, and future generations. Responsible innovation should prioritize transparency, accountability, and the minimization of harm, ensuring that the benefits of quantum computing are realized while mitigating potential risks.

Chapter 12: The Future of Computing: Integration and Evolution

12.1 Potential Coexistence and Integration of Classical and Quantum Computers

The future of computing may involve the coexistence and integration of classical and quantum computers, leveraging the strengths of both paradigms.

Hybrid Systems

Hybrid systems that combine classical and quantum computing elements can optimize performance for specific tasks. For example, classical computers can handle routine operations and control quantum processors, while quantum computers tackle complex computations that benefit from quantum speedups. This integration can enhance the capabilities of both types of computers, providing more efficient and powerful computing solutions.

Interoperability

Developing interoperability between classical and quantum systems is crucial for seamless integration. Standardized protocols, interfaces, and software frameworks can facilitate the interaction between classical and quantum components, enabling the efficient transfer of data and execution of hybrid algorithms.

12.2 Hybrid Systems and Their Applications

Hybrid systems have the potential to revolutionize various fields by combining the best of classical and quantum computing.

Scientific Research

In scientific research, hybrid systems can accelerate simulations and data analysis, enabling breakthroughs in fields such as physics, chemistry, and biology. For example, classical computers can manage large datasets and perform preliminary analyses, while quantum computers execute detailed simulations and solve complex equations.

Artificial Intelligence

Hybrid systems can enhance artificial intelligence by combining classical machine learning techniques with quantum algorithms. This approach can improve the training and optimization of AI models, leading to more accurate predictions and efficient problem-solving.

Optimization and Logistics

Hybrid systems can tackle optimization problems in logistics, transportation, and supply chain management. Classical computers can handle data collection and initial analysis, while quantum algorithms provide optimal solutions to complex logistical challenges.

12.3 Speculations on the Long-Term Evolution of Computing Technology

The long-term evolution of computing technology may bring about transformative changes in how we interact with and utilize computers.

Advances in Quantum Computing

As quantum computing technology matures, we may see the development of more scalable and reliable quantum processors, capable of solving a broader range of problems. Advances in qubit coherence, error correction, and quantum algorithms will drive the practical application of quantum computing in various industries.

Emerging Technologies

The evolution of computing may also involve the emergence of new technologies, such as neuromorphic computing, which mimics the brain's neural networks, and photonic computing, which uses light for data processing. These technologies have the potential to complement and enhance both classical and quantum computing, leading to new paradigms and capabilities.

Societal Impact

The continued advancement of computing technology will have profound societal impacts, influencing how we work, communicate, and solve global challenges. Ensuring responsible innovation and addressing ethical considerations will be crucial to maximizing the benefits and minimizing the risks associated with these technological advancements.

Conclusion

The comparison between quantum computers and traditional computers highlights the unique strengths and challenges of each paradigm. While traditional computers have revolutionized society and driven technological progress, quantum computers offer the potential to solve problems that are currently intractable. The future of computing lies in the integration and evolution of both technologies, harnessing their complementary capabilities to address complex challenges and unlock new possibilities. As we continue to explore and develop these technologies, responsible innovation and ethical considerations will be essential to shaping a future where computing serves the greater good.

Chapter 13: Preparing for the Quantum Future

13.1 Education and Workforce Development

To fully harness the potential of quantum computing, a well-prepared workforce and educated populace are essential.

Educational Initiatives

Educational institutions need to incorporate quantum computing into their curricula. This includes offering specialized courses in quantum mechanics, quantum algorithms, and quantum hardware. Interdisciplinary programs that combine computer science, physics, and engineering will prepare students for careers in quantum computing.

Professional Training

Workforce development programs should focus on reskilling and upskilling professionals. Providing training in quantum programming languages, such as Qiskit, Cirq, and others, can help current IT professionals transition into quantum computing roles. Online courses, workshops, and certification programs can make these opportunities accessible to a broader audience.

Collaboration Between Academia and Industry

Strong partnerships between academia and industry can drive innovation and practical applications. Collaborative research projects, internships, and industry-sponsored programs can provide students and professionals with hands-on experience and exposure to cutting-edge quantum technologies.

13.2 Policy and Regulation

The development and deployment of quantum computing technologies will require thoughtful policy and regulatory frameworks.

Data Security and Privacy

Governments and regulatory bodies need to develop policies that address the security implications of quantum computing. This includes creating standards for quantum-resistant encryption and ensuring that data privacy laws evolve to protect against new threats.

Funding and Support

Government funding and support for quantum research and development are crucial. Public investments in quantum computing can accelerate technological advancements and ensure that countries remain competitive in the global landscape.

Ethical Guidelines

Establishing ethical guidelines for the development and use of quantum technologies is essential. These guidelines should address issues such as data privacy, security, and equitable access, ensuring that the benefits of quantum computing are distributed fairly and responsibly.

13.3 Public Awareness and Engagement

Raising public awareness and fostering engagement with quantum computing can help demystify the technology and build public support.

Public Outreach

Initiatives such as public lectures, documentaries, and science festivals can educate the public about quantum computing and its potential impact. Simplifying complex concepts and highlighting real-world applications can make the technology more accessible and interesting to a broader audience.

Citizen Science Projects

Citizen science projects that involve the public in quantum computing research can foster interest and engagement. Platforms that allow individuals to contribute to quantum experiments or simulations can provide hands-on learning experiences and promote a sense of participation in scientific discovery.

Media and Communication

The media plays a crucial role in shaping public perception of quantum computing. Accurate and balanced reporting on advancements, challenges, and ethical considerations can help inform and engage the public. Encouraging scientists and experts to communicate their work effectively can also bridge the gap between research and public understanding.

13.4 Future Research Directions

Ongoing research is vital to overcome the current challenges and unlock the full potential of quantum computing.

Scalability and Error Correction

Researchers are focusing on developing scalable quantum processors and improving error correction methods. Advances in qubit technology, such as topological qubits and new materials, will be key to building larger, more reliable quantum computers.

Algorithm Development

The development of new quantum algorithms is essential to expanding the range of applications for quantum computing. Research in areas such as quantum machine learning, quantum optimization, and quantum simulations will drive innovation and practical use cases.

Interdisciplinary Research

Interdisciplinary research that combines quantum computing with fields such as biology, chemistry, and material science can lead to groundbreaking discoveries. Collaborations across disciplines can uncover new applications and push the boundaries of what quantum computing can achieve.

13.5 Preparing for Disruption and Transformation

The advent of quantum computing will bring about significant changes across various sectors. Preparing for this disruption is essential for a smooth transition.

Industry Adaptation

Industries need to assess the potential impact of quantum computing on their operations and strategies. This includes identifying areas where quantum computing can provide competitive advantages and investing in research and development to stay ahead of the curve.

Economic Implications

The economic implications of quantum computing, including job creation, market shifts, and new business models, need to be carefully managed. Policymakers and business leaders should work together to ensure that the transition to a quantum-enabled economy is inclusive and equitable.

Social Impact

Understanding and addressing the social impact of quantum computing is crucial. This includes considering how the technology will affect employment, education, and access to services. Proactive measures can help mitigate negative effects and ensure that the benefits of quantum computing are widely shared.

Conclusion: Embracing the Quantum Future

Quantum computing represents a profound shift in the landscape of technology, offering unprecedented opportunities and challenges. As we stand on the brink of this new era, it is essential to approach the development and deployment of quantum computing with foresight, responsibility, and a commitment to inclusivity.

Innovation and Collaboration

Innovation in quantum computing will be driven by collaboration across disciplines, sectors, and borders. By fostering partnerships and encouraging open research, we can accelerate progress and overcome the challenges that lie ahead.

Responsible Development

Responsible development of quantum computing requires careful consideration of ethical, social, and economic impacts. Ensuring that the technology is developed and used in ways that benefit society as a whole will be key to its successful integration.

Future Prospects

The future of computing, enriched by the power of quantum technologies, holds immense promise. From solving complex scientific problems to revolutionizing industries, quantum computing has the potential to transform our world in ways we are only beginning to imagine.

By embracing the potential of quantum computing and preparing for its impact, we can navigate the transition to this new era with confidence and optimism, unlocking new possibilities and creating a better future for all.

Book Summary

Quantum Computers Vs Traditional Computers

Table of Contents

Chapter 1: Introduction to Computing

1.1 Overview of Traditional Computing

- Definition and scope of traditional computing
- Key historical milestones in classical computing
- Evolution from early mechanical devices to modern digital computers

1.2 Introduction to Quantum Computing

- Definition and scope of quantum computing
- Early theoretical foundations and pioneers in the field
- The journey from theoretical physics to practical quantum computers

1.3 Importance of Comparing the Two Paradigms

- Why understanding both paradigms is crucial for future technological advancements
- The potential implications for various industries
- The broader impact on science, technology, and society

Chapter 2: Foundations of Traditional Computing

2.1 Historical Development

- The origins of computing: From abacuses to early mechanical calculators

- The advent of electronic computing: ENIAC and beyond
- The rise of personal computers and the internet revolution

2.2 Basic Principles and Architecture

- The binary system and Boolean logic
- The von Neumann architecture: CPU, memory, and storage
- The role of operating systems and software in classical computing

2.3 Key Components: CPU, Memory, Storage, and I/O Devices

- The central processing unit (CPU): Function and design
- Types of memory: RAM, cache, and long-term storage
- Input and output devices: Keyboards, monitors, and peripheral devices

Chapter 3: Fundamentals of Quantum Computing

3.1 Historical Context and Key Milestones

- Early quantum mechanics and its implications for computing
- Theoretical contributions from Richard Feynman, David Deutsch, and others
- Experimental breakthroughs and the current state of quantum computing

3.2 Quantum Mechanics Principles: Superposition, Entanglement, and Quantum Tunneling

- The principle of superposition and its computational advantages
- Quantum entanglement: A unique resource for quantum information processing
- Quantum tunneling and its role in quantum computing

3.3 Basic Components: Qubits, Quantum Gates, and Quantum Circuits

- The nature and types of qubits: Photonic, superconducting, and trapped ions
- Quantum gates: Basic operations and their equivalents to classical logic gates
- Building and operating quantum circuits for complex computations

Chapter 4: Bit vs. Qubit: The Core Difference

4.1 Understanding Classical Bits

- The binary digit: Definition and properties
- How bits are used in traditional computing for data representation and processing
- The limitations of binary logic in classical computing

4.2 Exploring Qubits and Their Unique Properties

- The concept of a qubit: Representing 0 and 1 simultaneously
- Quantum superposition and its implications for parallelism
- Quantum entanglement and its potential for correlated computations

4.3 The Impact of Superposition and Entanglement on Computation

- How superposition allows quantum computers to process multiple possibilities at once
- The role of entanglement in enhancing computational power and speed
- Practical examples demonstrating the power of qubits over classical bits

Chapter 5: Computational Models: Classical vs. Quantum

5.1 Turing Machines and Classical Algorithms

- The Turing machine model and its significance in classical computing
- An overview of classical algorithms: Sorting, searching, and optimization
- Limitations of classical algorithms in solving complex problems

5.2 Quantum Turing Machines and Quantum Algorithms

- The concept of a quantum Turing machine
- Key quantum algorithms: Shor's algorithm for factoring, Grover's algorithm for search
- Theoretical and practical advantages of quantum algorithms

5.3 Key Differences in Problem-Solving Approaches

- Deterministic vs. probabilistic computation
- How quantum algorithms can solve certain problems exponentially faster
- Case studies highlighting the strengths and weaknesses of each paradigm

Chapter 6: Processing and Speed: A Comparative Analysis

6.1 Classical Processing: Sequential and Parallel Computing

- The nature of sequential processing in classical computers
- Parallel processing and multi-core CPUs
- Limitations of classical processing power and efficiency

6.2 Quantum Processing: Parallelism Through Superposition

- How superposition enables massive parallelism in quantum

computing

- Examples of quantum speedup in specific problems
- Theoretical and experimental comparisons of processing speeds

6.3 Performance Benchmarks and Potential Speed Advantages

- Current benchmarks for classical and quantum computers
- Potential speed advantages in cryptography, optimization, and simulation
- Challenges in achieving and maintaining quantum speed advantages

Chapter 7: Algorithms: Classical and Quantum Perspectives

7.1 Overview of Classical Algorithms

- Fundamental algorithms: Sorting, searching, and graph algorithms
- Complexity classes: P, NP, and beyond
- Real-world applications and limitations of classical algorithms

7.2 Introduction to Quantum Algorithms: Shor's Algorithm, Grover's Algorithm

- Shor's algorithm: Breaking RSA encryption and its significance
- Grover's algorithm: Speeding up database searches
- Other notable quantum algorithms and their applications

7.3 Comparative Efficiency and Real-World Implications

- Efficiency metrics for classical vs. quantum algorithms
- Practical implications for industry and research
- The future of algorithm development in a quantum era

Chapter 8: Applications of Traditional Computing

8.1   Everyday   Applications: Personal   Computing,   Business, Entertainment

- Personal computing: Operating systems, applications, and the internet
- Business computing: ERP, CRM, and data management
- Entertainment: Gaming, multimedia, and virtual reality

8.2   High-Performance   Computing: Scientific   Simulations,   Data Analysis

- The role of supercomputers in scientific research
- Big data analytics and machine learning
- Case studies of high-performance computing applications

8.3 Limitations and Challenges Faced by Traditional Computers

- Computational limits: P vs. NP problems
- Energy consumption and heat dissipation
- The end of Moore's Law and the search for new paradigms

Chapter 9: Potential Applications of Quantum Computing

9.1   Cryptography   and   Security: Breaking   Classical   Encryption, Quantum Encryption

- How quantum computing can break current encryption methods
- Quantum encryption techniques: Quantum key distribution
- Implications for data security and privacy

9.2 Optimization Problems: Logistics, Finance, Machine Learning

- Quantum solutions to complex optimization problems

- Applications in logistics, finance, and supply chain management
- Potential breakthroughs in machine learning and AI

9.3 Scientific Research: Quantum Simulations, Drug Discovery, Material Science

- Quantum simulations of chemical and physical systems
- Accelerating drug discovery and personalized medicine
- Advancements in material science and new material development

Chapter 10: Hardware and Technical Requirements

10.1 Traditional Computer Hardware: Transistors, Integrated Circuits, Moore's Law

- The evolution of classical computer hardware
- The impact of Moore's Law on hardware development
- Current state and future trends in traditional hardware

10.2 Quantum Hardware: Qubits, Quantum Processors, Error Correction

- Types of qubits and their physical implementations
- The architecture of quantum processors
- Error correction methods and the challenge of quantum decoherence

10.3 Challenges in Developing and Maintaining Quantum Computers

- Technical challenges: Qubit coherence, scalability, and stability
- The need for extreme cooling and isolation
- The roadmap to practical and scalable quantum computers

Chapter 11: Current State of Technology and Research

11.1 Advances in Traditional Computing: AI, Machine Learning, Cloud Computing

- Recent advancements in artificial intelligence and machine learning
- The role of cloud computing in expanding computational capabilities
- Future trends in traditional computing technology

11.2 Current State of Quantum Computing: Leading Companies, Experimental Achievements

- Overview of leading companies and research institutions in quantum computing
- Key experimental achievements and breakthroughs
- The current landscape of quantum computing technology

11.3 Major Research Initiatives and Future Prospects

- Government and private sector research initiatives
- The potential timeline for achieving practical quantum computing
- Future prospects and emerging trends in quantum research

Chapter 12: Societal and Ethical Implications

12.1 Impact of Traditional Computing on Society: Jobs, Privacy, Digital Divide

- The transformative impact of classical computing on society
- Issues of privacy, security, and data ethics
- The digital divide and efforts to bridge the gap

12.2 Potential Societal Impact of Quantum Computing: Data Security, Economic Shifts

- How quantum computing could revolutionize data security
- Potential economic shifts and new industries
- Ethical considerations and the need for responsible innovation

12.3 Ethical Considerations in the Development and Deployment of Quantum Technology

- Balancing innovation with ethical responsibility
- Ensuring equitable access to quantum technology
- The role of policy and regulation in guiding quantum development

Chapter 13: The Future of Computing: Integration and Evolution

13.1 Potential Coexistence and Integration of Classical and Quantum Computers

- Scenarios for the coexistence of classical and quantum computers
- How hybrid systems could leverage the strengths of both paradigms
- Practical examples of integrated computing solutions

13.2 Hybrid Systems and Their Applications

- The architecture and design of hybrid computing systems
- Applications in scientific research, industry, and beyond
- Case studies of successful hybrid computing implementations

13.3 Speculations on the Long-Term Evolution of Computing Technology

- The potential long-term impact of quantum computing on technology and society
- Emerging technologies that could shape the future of computing
- Speculative visions of a post-quantum computing era

About the Author

Arief Muinnudin was born in Malaysia in 1987, where he discovered his passion for writing at a young age. Growing up surrounded by the diverse cultures and vibrant landscapes of Malaysia, Arief developed a deep appreciation for storytelling and the power of words to connect people from different backgrounds.

From his early years, Arief was drawn to literature and the art of crafting narratives that captivate and inspire readers. He immersed himself in a wide range of genres, from fiction to non-fiction, exploring various themes and styles to hone his writing skills.

As Arief's love for writing blossomed, so did his ambition to share meaningful stories with the world. He embarked on a journey to become a published author, dedicating countless hours to researching, writing, and refining his manuscripts.

With each book he wrote, Arief aimed to engage readers on a profound level, sparking discussions, provoking thought, and leaving a lasting impact on their lives. His commitment to creating compelling and insightful content earned him recognition as a talented writer with a unique voice and perspective.

Arief's passion for literature continues to drive him forward, inspiring him to explore new ideas, tackle challenging topics, and connect with readers on a deeper level through the power of storytelling.

Read more at https://ariefebook.etsy.com.